understanding
citizenship 1

Tony Thorpe

CITIZENSHIP
FOUNDATION

Hodder & Stoughton

A MEMBER OF THE HODDER HEADLINE GROUP

In this series we have, to the best of our knowledge, described the law as it stood on 1 December 2000. However, in trying to summarise and simplify the law we have had to leave out some legal details. Therefore, this book cannot be taken as proof of your legal rights. We stongly recommend that you seek further advice before taking any legal action.

The Citizenship Foundation is an independent educational charity, which aims to help people become more effective citizens through a better understanding of law and society. It produces the Young Citizen's Passport, a practical pocket guide to the law, which can be used in conjunction with this book.
Further details of this and information about its other activities and teaching materials can be found on the Citizenship Foundation's website at www.citfou.org.uk.
The Citizenship Foundation, Ferroners House, Shaftesbury Place (off Aldersgate Street), London EC2Y 8AA, tel 020 7367 0500, fax 020 7367 0501, E-mail info@citfou.org.uk.

Editors: Jan Newton and Don Rowe

Orders: please contact Bookpoint Ltd, 78 Milton Park, Abingdon, Oxon OX14 4TD.
Telephone: (44) 01235 827720, Fax: (44) 01235 400454.
Lines are open from 9.00am - 6.00pm, Monday to Saturday, with a 24 hour message answering service.
E-mail address: orders@bookpoint.co.uk.

The editors and author would like to thank Dan Mace, Vikki Carter and Caroline Hadfield for their help in preparing and checking the accuracy of the text in this book, and to those teachers who commented upon the draft text - particularly Jackie Fitch, Icknield High School, Luton: Will Ord, Cockermouth School, Cumbria; Sairah Shah, The Charter School, London; Alan Shaw, Brownhills High School, Stoke on Trent; Steve Staerck, The Cedars School, Leighton Buzzard.

Also to Fiona Dodwell and the Hitchin British Schools Trust; Pattie Hill and the Education Welfare Service, Solihull Metropolitan Borough Council; Councillor Roy Miller, Milton Keynes Metropolitan Borough Council; Thorpe St Andrew School, Norwich; West Yorkshire Trading Standards Office.

The publishers would like to thank the following individuals, institutions and companies for permission to reproduce copyright illustrations in this book:
Corbis, 3, 26 (bottom), 37 (top), 57 (middle), 62; Digital Vision, 16 (bottom left), 18 (bottom), 27 (middle), 28,29,30; Mary Evans Picture Library, 18 (left), 21 (bottom right); Eyewire, 9 (top), 23; The Stephen Lawrence Trust 45 (bottom right); PhotoDisc, 3, 4, 5, 6, 7, 10, 11,13, 15, 16 (top & bottom), 17, 19, 20, 21(top), 22 (bottom left & right), 25, 26, 27, 28, 29, 30, 31, 33, 34, 37 (middle, bottom) , 41, 44, 47, 49, 50, 57 (top, right), 58, 61, 62; The Press Association 22 (top, left and right), 54 (top), 63 (bottom); Paula Solloway/Format 32 (bottom right); Telegraph Colour Library, 35 (middle), 46 (bottom); Universal Pictorial Press & Agency Ltd - Scales of Justice image.

British Library Cataloguing in Publication Data.
A catalogue record for this title is available from The British Library.

ISBN 0 340 78077 0

First published 2001
Impression number 10 9 8 7 6 5 4 3 2 1
Year   2005 2004 2003 2002 2001

Copyright © 2001 The Citizenship Foundation

Design and artwork by Nomad Graphique.
Printed in Italy for Hodder & Stoughton Educational, a division of Hodder Headline Plc, 338 Euston Road, London NW1 3BH, by Printer Trento.

Contents

Learning

04   What are schools for?

10   School rules

Growing up

16   Parents

20   Punishment

24   Rights and responsibilities

Keeping safe

30   Bullying

34   Right and wrong

36   Crime

42   Racism

Taking care

46   Working Lives

52   Trading standards

56   Driving lessons

60   All in the game

What are schools for?

In this unit we look at some of the reasons for going to school.

No school today

Truancy

In England and Wales, just under nine million children of all ages go to school. Government figures showed that in the year 2000 about 65,000 children had what is called an unauthorised absence. This means that they were away from school without any obvious good reason.

Playing truant

Gemma Ashton started to play truant during her first year at secondary school. Until then, her attendance had been good. Sometimes she went into town and met a friend, but she usually stayed at home. She liked reading, she watched television and often did some cooking. It wasn't that Gemma didn't like school. She just didn't see much point in going.

After Gemma had been away for almost a term, Mrs Ellis, the education welfare officer, called round. It was the first of many visits she paid to Gemma's house, as she tried to

convince Gemma and her mum and dad of the need for her to go to school. On some days Mrs Ellis came to take her to school, but Gemma would hide in the garden or upstairs and her mum or dad would tell Mrs Ellis that they thought she had already left. Mrs Ellis tried to get Gemma into another school. Gemma agreed to go for an interview, but didn't turn up.

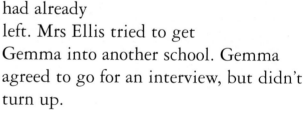

A visit from the education welfare officer

After many warnings, the local authority decided to prosecute Mr and Mrs Ashton for not making sure that Gemma was properly educated. They were found guilty and fined £250. But Gemma's truancy continued.

Arrangements were made for Gemma to see an **educational psychologist**. The report said that she was of average intelligence. Her reading and writing were good, but her maths was weak – probably because she had missed so much time from school. But the thing that worried the psychologist most was the damage being caused by Gemma seeing so few young people of her own age.

In Year 7, Gemma was absent two or three times a week. By Year 9, she was at school on only eight or nine days each term. Gemma is now 14 and in Year 10. She says that she wants to go to art college.

Gemma has now been placed in care by a court, because she missed so much time from school. Someone from the home where she lives now takes her to school everyday.

Key**Words**

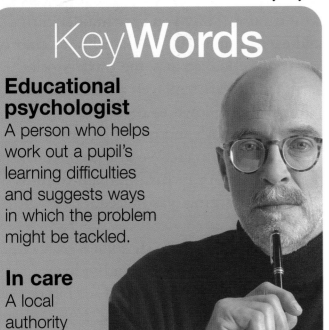

Educational psychologist
A person who helps work out a pupil's learning difficulties and suggests ways in which the problem might be tackled.

In care
A local authority applies to a court to take a child into care when it feels that the child is suffering some kind of serious harm and that it would be better if the child were looked after elsewhere.

? Questions

1 What do you think Gemma has missed by being away from school so much?

2 Why do you think Gemma's parents allowed her to stay away from school?

3 What do you think should happen to Gemma? Do you think she should be made to go to school?

The law

Parents have a legal duty to make sure that their children are educated, and this usually means going to school. If they don't do this, they may be committing a criminal offence and can be fined. In law, it is no excuse for parents to say that they didn't realise that their child was not at school or that they could not do anything to make them attend. Parents can be sent to special guidance sessions to help them make sure their child attends school. If this fails, the local authority can apply to take the child into care.

Educational welfare officers have the job of helping pupils and persuading them that they should be in school. A police officer who finds a child in a public place, and believes that he or she should be in school, also has the power to take the child back to school.

What are schools for?

Home time

A steadily increasing number of children don't go to school at all. It's not because they are ill or playing truant, it's because for some particular reason their parents have decided to educate them at home.

There are no official records giving details of the numbers of children who learn at home, but organisations that help parents to teach their children estimate that about 10,000 families in the United Kingdom now educate their children at home.

why we get thunderstorm

School's out

Ten-year-old Lydia has never been to school, apart from two weeks in a nursery class when she was four. Lydia's classroom is the front room of her house and her teacher is her dad. While Lydia's mum is out at work, Lydia and her sister Lauren (8) and brother Lenny (6) are working on a project with their dad.

Unlike ordinary school, Lydia's work is not divided into separate subjects. 'I give them a question,' says Mick, Lydia's dad, 'and get them to tell me ways in which we can answer it.

'We recently did some work on the weather. Finding out why it rains. Why you get thunderstorms and even simple things like why it's cold in winter. We looked at some travel stories where the weather played an important part, we went down to the library for geography books and took some weather readings of our own. We also went to the Science Museum in Birmingham to find out how lightning was caused.'

Mick was in the navy. He's not a teacher. 'I want to give my children individual attention and I don't want to force them into a certain way of thinking. I want them to think for themselves,' he explains. 'I think they can be happier here than at school. There's no competition or bullying. There's also time to talk about questions of right and wrong.'

Mick has had several visits from local education officers, checking to see that Lydia and her brothers are being properly educated. 'I was nervous when I started,' says Mick, 'but now I think it's going quite well. Lydia might do her GCSE maths next year and eventually wants to join the navy to train to be a diver.'

The law

The law says that it is the duty of any parent with a child aged between 5 and 16 to make sure that their child receives what is called an efficient full-time education by, 'either regular attendance at school or otherwise'. The word *otherwise* is interesting because it means that children don't actually have to go to school. The important thing is that they get a good education. This is why children can be educated at home by their parents.

? Questions

1 What do you think it would be like to be educated at home? What do you think would be the advantages and disadvantages?

HOME SWEET HOME!

2 In a year's time Lydia will be old enough to go to secondary school. Do you think she should continue to be educated at home?

3 What are the differences between the cases of Lydia and Gemma, on the previous page?

4 The law allows parents to educate their children at home. Do you think this should be changed? Give reasons for your answer.

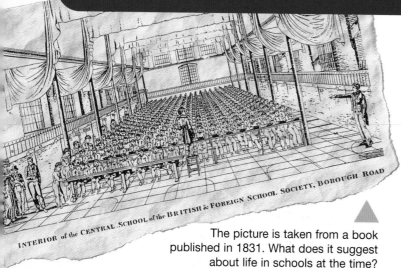

The picture is taken from a book published in 1831. What does it suggest about life in schools at the time?

The way we were

Compulsory education

It wasn't until 1870 that education became **compulsory** for most children in England and Wales. Until then, schools were mainly run by the Church or by **charities**. Attendance was **voluntary**. Children didn't have to go to school, although many did, just staying long enough to learn how to read and write and to do some simple maths.

Many classes were large, and the teachers could be harsh and brutal. Children were taught to read using the Bible, often by repeating certain phrases over and over again.

If you had asked anyone at that time why children should go to school, they would probably have given you two reasons. The first was that children needed to be able to read and write to do a job. The second was that they needed to be taught how to behave properly. In the mid 1800s, a lot of adults were worried about the hooliganism and misbehaviour of young people.

From 1870, children were expected to be in school from the age of five, until they were eleven. (Since then, the school leaving age has been raised to 14, 15 and then 16, in 1972.) Attendance was compulsory, although action was not always taken against boys and girls who didn't go to school. Although teachers wanted the children to be in school because their pay depended on good attendance, factory owners and landowners often encouraged children to stay away and work in the factories or fields. Children were a good source of cheap labour.

? Questions

1 Think of all the things that people today learn during their time at school. How different is this from 100 years ago?

2 Is there anything that schools ought to be teaching that they are not, in your opinion? Could schools help young people more?

Time for school?

Children living in England, Wales and Scotland must go to school between the ages of 5 and 16. In Northern Ireland they start school aged 4, and continue until they are 16. In other countries the pattern is different.

Country	Children must go to school between
Australia	6–15 yrs
Bangladesh	6–10 yrs
France	5–16 yrs
Germany	6–15 yrs
India	5–14 yrs
Italy	6–14 yrs
Norway	7–16 yrs
Poland	6–18 yrs
Trinidad and Tobago	6–12 yrs

Take five

Woodlands Primary School in Grimsby is different in one respect from almost every other school in the country. Their school year is divided not into three terms but into five. Instead of working for three terms of 12 or 14 weeks, they work in five eight-week blocks. They have two-week breaks in between, and four weeks off in the summer.

The head teacher says that a lot of the resources in other schools lie idle at present, particularly in the long summer holidays when they are closed. The five-term arrangement, he feels, helps pupils and teachers pace themselves better. More frequent breaks mean that everyone is less drained and more rested.

3 How much schooling do you think we need? Some people feel that children should start school earlier. Others say it should be later. What do you think? How would you decide whether we ought to change the ages at which everyone must go to school?

4 How would you feel about changing to a four- or five-term school year? What do you think would be the advantages and disadvantages? How should schools decide on the best thing to do?

KeyWords

Charities
Organisations that have been set up to help people in some kind of need or to do some good in the community.

Compulsory
Something that you have to do, usually by law.

Voluntary
Something that you choose to do.

School rules

In this unit we look at questions of fairness in school.

Speaking out

The news is out

Four pupils in Year 10 at a school in Nottinghamshire wrote to their local newspaper complaining that they were not being taught properly because their teachers were often away from school.

The newspaper was interested in the story and arranged an interview with the girls. 'Teachers always seem to be off sick and supply teachers don't know where we are with our work,' said one pupil, aged 15. Another added, 'They sometimes don't know what room they are supposed to be in and, when they do turn up, often don't have a key. All this wastes time. Most of us don't feel prepared for our exams next year.'

A few days later, the story was front-page news. 'Our exam grades at risk, warn pupils,' shouted the headlines. 'Students protest over "too many supply teachers".'

Questions

1 Do you think the pupils were right to get in touch with the newspaper? What else could they have done?

2 What do you think the head teacher should do? What sort of things does she need to think about?

Dealing with the problem

The phone started ringing at school as soon as the newspaper came out. Parents, governors and reporters from other newspapers all wanted to know what was happening. The head teacher told them that there was no problem. 'Staff absenteeism is no greater at this school than any other in the town,' she said.

The head teacher then spoke to the four pupils involved. She asked each of them to come to school with their parents and then to write a letter apologising for the damage that they had done to the school's reputation.

Three of the girls agreed to say sorry, but the fourth, Sarah, refused, saying, 'I didn't feel that I had done anything wrong.'

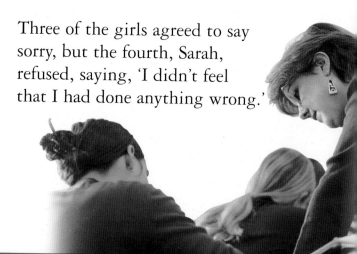

3 Was Sarah right to refuse to apologise, in your opinion?

4 How do you think the head teacher dealt with the matter? Could she have acted differently?

5 What do you think she should do now that Sarah has refused to say sorry?

The next step

Since Sarah had refused to apologise, the head teacher wrote to her parents telling them that Sarah would be excluded from school for 'bringing the school into disrepute' and because her behaviour could affect future pupil numbers.

The news of Sarah's **exclusion** soon reached the local newspaper and it was not long before her story appeared in national newspapers, on television and the radio.

 THINK! Do you think the head teacher was right to exclude Sarah from school? Read the law section opposite to help you make your decision.

How would you describe Sarah's behaviour? How easy is it to stand alone when no one else seems to agree with you?

Agreement is reached

It was almost the end of term when Sarah was excluded from school. Her parents wrote to the **governors** of the school asking for their daughter to be allowed to return. After a lot of discussion, the head teacher and governors agreed that Sarah could return at the start of the next term.

The law

Everyone has the right to free speech under the Human Rights Act – but rules can be made to prevent disorder and to protect others.

Schools should not exclude pupils unless they have done all that they can to deal with the problem. A pupil should be permanently excluded only if their staying in the school would seriously affect the education and safety of others.

School rules must be reasonable and must not be against the law.

6 Sarah's head teacher said that pupils should not criticise their school in public. Do you think this is a fair rule?

Key Words

Exclusion
Ordering a pupil to leave school permanently or for a set period of time.

Governors
Members of the local community, such as parents, teachers, politicians and business people, who have responsibility for the way in which a school is run.

School rules

Fair enough

Making the rules

Most people agree that school should be fair. But what does fairness mean? How does a school make sure that everyone – pupils, parents and staff – are treated fairly?

? Questions ?

1 Look at the rules for Prissick School. What do these rules tell us about life in England in 1846?

2 Which of the rules for the children and parents at Prissick School do you think are fair and which are unfair?

3 Do you think any of these rules should be introduced today?

⚜ Rules for Prissick School ⚜
Hartlepool, 1846

1 You must come clean and washed and combed to school at nine o'clock in the morning, to answer your names, to be present at prayers, and ready with your tasks.

2 You must not fight nor quarrel with any one, nor loiter in the streets.

3 You must do as you are told both at home and at school, and be obedient to your parents, teachers, and all your superiors.

4 You must speak politely to everybody, and do as you are told with good humour and cheerfulness.

5 Any child who is absent without leave, on the morning or evening of any day, pays a halfpenny for each time, that is to say, one penny for every day's absence; half that sum for being too late; but if absent on Sundays to forfeit twice that sum. The fines form a fund for rewarding monitors and assistant teachers.

6 All children must go to church every Sunday morning.

7 If any children are found guilty of lying, swearing, cursing, stealing, taking God's name in vain, profaning the Lord's Day, using any indecent language in the streets or elsewhere, they are corrected as the school decides.

Rules given to parents

1 You must always send your children to school, clean, washed and combed; and make sure they follow all the rules and regulations of the school.

2 You must make sure your children read the Holy Scriptures and say their prayers, morning and evening; so that both you and your children may be better informed of your duties towards God.

3 By your behaviour, you must set your children good examples; keep them in good order at home; and correct them for the faults they commit out of school, or inform the master or mistress thereof.

4 You must not allow your children to be seen with any mob, nor allow them to play at dice, pitchpenny, or other unlawful games, in the street or elsewhere.

Today, many schools ask all those people who are involved with the school to sign an agreement which sets out how everyone in the school should expect to be treated and how they should treat others. This is called a home-school agreement.

▼ A modern home-school agreement used by a school in Norfolk

As a student, I will:
- be polite and courteous to all,
- come to school regularly, maintain punctuality and be prepared for lessons with the necessary equipment,
- wear appropriate school attire,
- respect other people's property,
- accept responsibility for my actions.

As parents, we will:
- support our children by providing a loving and caring environment that actively supports the school,
- try to attend parent consultation evenings,
- ensure our children attend school regularly.

As staff, we will:
- treat all students with respect and value them equally,
- provide challenging programmes of study,
- strive to maintain an environment where we feel safe and secure,
- set and mark work within a reasonable time span.

4 How is the modern home-school agreement different from the rules Prissick School? Are they fair and reasonable?

5 How do you think schools should decide on their rules?

6 What advice would you give to teachers about rules in school?

7 What makes a rule fair or unfair, in your opinion?

The law

Schools must, by law, ask all parents to sign what is called a home–school agreement. This is a list of things that the school and parents agree to do to make sure that pupils are educated as well as possible.

Parents don't have to sign the agreement. A pupil should never be refused entry to a school because of this.

Mrs Dolman's day

Mrs Dolman teaches English and PE at Bracken High School. Last Thursday she taught all day and had a number of situations to deal with.

Look at each situation and try to decide:

what difficulty Mrs Dolman faces in each case, and what you think would be the *fairest* thing for her to do.

I let Luke, who's in Year 8, go to the toilet five minutes after the beginning of the first lesson. Three minutes later, his friend Carla asks if she can be excused.

In lesson two, James, who is in Year 9, reaches across and takes Maria's pencil case. Maria tries to get the case back and swears at James.

In lesson three, after break, I see Vijay, Year 7, eating a packet of crisps – although, like everyone else, he's getting on with his work.

I set my Year 10 class a test. Halfway through, Jane's mobile phone rings. The school asks pupils not to bring in mobile phones.

As I walk into the classroom at the start of lesson five I see a boy crouched on the floor, holding a handkerchief to his face, his nose badly bleeding. The boy says that Michael has just hit him. Michael says, 'He deserved it, Miss, he shouldn't say things like that about my family.'

The last lesson, is PE. Terry has forgotten his kit again. I think this is because some of the others in class make fun of him because he's not very good at sport.

School rules

Tuesday morning break

A quick repair

On Monday afternoon, Mr Evans, head of PE at Whinney Moor School, noticed that one of the small trampolines in the sports hall needed repairing. He decided to mend it himself after school, by replacing a three-metre length of elastic. On his way back to the main school building, Mr Evans wound the old elastic into a coil and placed it at the bottom of a waste bin, opposite the window where drinks and biscuits were sold from the tuck shop at break.

The following day at the start of morning break, Ashley, who was in Year 7, spotted the elastic, and took it out of the bin. For a couple of minutes he ran around flicking the end of the elastic at people's legs, but soon lost interest and tossed it back into the bin. This time, however, the elastic didn't fall to the bottom. About a metre was left draped over the side.

Almost immediately, the elastic was out of the bin again. This time it was taken by two boys, Scott and Mark, who were in Year 10. After stretching it as far as they could, Scott started to wind the elastic around Mark's waist. Sean, also in Year 10, was standing close by, eating a biscuit that he had just bought from the tuck shop. As Mark ran off with the elastic round his waist, it started to unravel. With Scott still holding on to one end, the elastic flicked up and hit Sean in the eye.

The injury to Sean's eye was very serious. His sight was permanently damaged.

The two teachers on duty that morning were still clearing students out of the classrooms when the accident happened.

 THINK! Who do you think was responsible for Sean's injury? Write down the names of those who you feel had some part in this.

In court

Sean's parents believed that the school was responsible for the accident and decided to take the **local education authority**, which ran the school, to court.

If the judge could be convinced that the school was at fault, Sean would receive **compensation** for the injury to his eye.

Everybody agreed on the facts of the case. They also agreed that discipline at Whinney Moor School was very good.

However, the **barrister** who put the case

on behalf of Sean's mum and dad said that Mr Evans should have realised that there would be a problem in leaving the elastic in the bin by the tuck shop. Mr Evans also said that the school was not providing proper supervision at break time.

THINK!

Do you think Mr Evans should have known that leaving the elastic in the bin would cause a problem? Is there any evidence to show that he realised it could be a danger?

What would you decide in this case, if you were the judge? Did Mr Evans and Whinney Moor School fail to carry out their responsibilities and did this cause the injury to Sean's eye?

Justice

The judge decided that Mr Evans should not have left the elastic in the bin. He said that the teacher should have realised that pupils would find it. Sean was awarded over £3,000 in compensation. As this case happened some time ago this would be about £35,000 in today's money.

? Questions

1 What do you think about this case? Was it right that Mr Evans and the school were found responsible? Were Ashley, Mark and Scott old enough to realise that what they were doing was dangerous?

2 What other parts of school life could be unsafe or dangerous in some way?

The law

Schools have a legal duty to do as much as they reasonably can to make sure that pupils are safe while they are in school.

Pupils also have a legal duty to behave in a reasonable and sensible way.

KeyWords

Barrister
A lawyer who is specially trained to present and argue a person's case in court. In most courts a barrister will wear a wig and gown.

Compensation
When a person is injured by the action of someone else, they can be awarded a sum of money to make up for loss or damage they have suffered. This is usually called compensation or damages.

Local education authority
Part of a local or county council responsible for providing schools for children living in the area.

Parents

In this unit we look at some of the rights and responsibilities of being a parent and think about how parents should deal with certain problems.

Being a parent

Missing

On Wednesday morning, Tanya opened her money box to discover that it was empty. There had been £25 in it at the weekend, and now there was nothing. Tanya went into the kitchen to tell her mum and dad, who asked if she had spent it or given it to anyone else. It wasn't long before the finger of suspicion pointed towards Tanya's younger sister, Zoë, aged 10. Zoë admitted that she had taken the money to give to two of her friends, and had kept a little bit back for herself.

 What do you think Tanya's mum and dad should do?
THINK!

Zoë agreed to pay the money back at a rate of £5 a month. A week later, £5 was missing from Zoë's mum's purse. Zoë was suspected straightaway and when she confessed, her mum was furious. She was determined to make her daughter realise that stealing was wrong.

The following day, Zoë's dad found a £10 note on the floor of Zoë's bedroom. When his daughter came back from school, he asked her where the money had come from. This time it took longer for her to confess, but eventually Zoë said that she had taken the money from a friend who'd come to stay at the weekend.

 What do you think Zoë's mum and dad should do now? Should Zoë be punished or helped?
THINK!

Zoë explained that she'd taken the money to pay back her mum and her sister. That evening Zoë's dad took Zoë to her friend's house to return the money, with a letter of apology. Treats were stopped and Zoë was banned from swimming, her favourite pastime, for three weeks.

Zoë said she had taken the money from a friend

There were no more problems for the next few days, until the telephone rang, late in the afternoon. It was the manager of a shop in town. Zoë had called in on the way home from school and had been caught trying to leave with a CD that she hadn't paid for.

Does an advert like this really sum up what parenting entails?

? Questions

1 Why do you think Zoë might have been behaving like this?

2 What are Zoë's parents' responsibilities in this situation?

3 How can they help Zoë best?

What makes a good parent?

Most parents will say that being a mum or dad can sometimes be the most difficult job in the world. There's no training, a lot of guesswork and you often make mistakes.

Being a parent for many people today is, in some ways, different from what it was in the past. Our families now tend to be smaller. One of the parents may live alone with their child and we are less likely to live either with or near our relatives. This means that grandparents and aunts and uncles may not be on hand to give advice and help out with the children.

Some people believe that being a parent is too important to be left to chance. They say that children need parenting lessons at school and that more help with family problems should be available to parents.

4 What do you think young people need from their parents?

5 What kind of problems can make it difficult to be a parent?

6 Do you think there should be classes in parenting at school? What should be included in these lessons?

The law

Children are responsible for the crimes that they commit from the age of 10. Parents are generally not responsible for the crimes their children commit.

Parents

Having a voice

Father's day

In the nineteenth century parents, particularly fathers, had the legal right to control much of their children's lives. Sometimes, it seems, parents treated children as if they were a piece of property.

Mr and Mrs Ellis were married in 1864. It does not appear to have been a happy marriage and they could not agree whether their three children should be brought up as Roman Catholics or Anglicans. When Mr Ellis decided to take the children away from their mother, his wife could do nothing to stop him. She was allowed to visit them once a month, and all letters between them were checked by Mr Ellis.

When their second child, Harriet, was 16, she asked to spend her holidays with her mother. Mr Ellis refused. Harriet and her mother tried to have this decision overturned by a court, but the judge decided that Mr Ellis was in the right. As long as he had not done anything wrong, the court had no power to interfere in how he chose to bring up his child.

? Questions

1 What kind of father do you imagine Mr Ellis was?

2 What advice would you give him if he were a parent today?

Deciding for the best

It is difficult for many parents to know when to let their children make decisions for themselves – especially if this means that the child might do something that the parents disapprove of, or which puts the child at risk.

3 How do you think a parent today should deal with disagreements with their child? Look at each of the following cases and decide what you think the parents should do.

Sarah 13, is given some money by her mum to buy a new top to wear to a party. She comes back with something that hardly covers her chest. Her mum and dad think it is much too revealing.

Mark 14, is told by his mum and dad that he has to go with them to his aunt's wedding. He doesn't want to go. He says that he won't know anyone, he doesn't like his aunt and he'd much rather stay at home by himself.

Jessica 11, decides to stop eating meat. Her mum disapproves and feels it will make life much harder having to prepare separate meals for her.

David 12, is spending a lot of time with his new friend Ross. David's mum wants him to get to know some other friends. She thinks Ross is a very bad influence.

Laura 13, has been going out with Jason, who is 19, for three weeks. Laura's mum and dad have just found out and think that Jason is too old for Laura.

Daniel 16, has been saving up for a motorbike for nearly three years. Now he's seen a second-hand one, which he can afford. His mum won't let him buy it. Many years ago, her brother was killed in a motorcycle accident. He was the same age as Daniel.

4 What would you say to someone who will soon become a parent for the first time about how they should bring up their child? What would you advise them **not** to do?

The law

There is no one law in England and Wales that lists all the rights and duties of parents. Governments have felt it would not be a good idea to try to list everything that parents should and should not do.

Instead, the law just says that parents have **parental responsibility** for their child. This means that they must behave and look after their child in a way that is in the child's best interests.

If there is a serious problem, and the case comes to court, the judge should base their decision on what they believe to be in the best interests of the child.

Parents who are married both have parental responsibility for their children, and this continues if the couple separate or divorce.

The situation for parents who are not married when their child is born is slightly different. A mother automatically has parental responsibility, but a father needs to apply for this, if he is to take part in decisions about how the child is brought up. With the mother's agreement, this can be done soon after the child is born, or can be applied for later, through a court.

In Scotland the law says that, if a child is not living with their parent, it is the duty of the parent to maintain personal relations and contact with their child on a regular basis.

Key Words

Parental responsibility

The responsibility and authority to care for a child's physical, moral and emotional needs.

Punishment

In this unit we look at ways in which parents discipline their children and ask whether it is right for a parent to hit a child.

How far should you go?

Everyone has been punished at some time in their life and their first experience of this is usually at home.

The end of the day

It's eight o'clock at night. I've had a bad day at work and my two young daughters don't want to go to bed. As I try to make her clean her teeth, Lauren, who is 6, flings her toothbrush across the bathroom and it falls into the toilet. She thinks this is funny (which it probably is) and her little sister Amy, who is 4, decides to copy her — and then flushes the toilet. One of the brushes disappears. The other stays floating in the pan.

 THINK! What do you think Lauren and Amy's mum or dad should do in this situation? Is there anything they should not do, in your opinion?

Points of view: Is it OK to smack a child?

Valerie: It depends what you mean by smacking. I don't mean beating a child with a stick, but sometimes a quick slap on the leg is absolutely necessary. It does no harm. It passes quickly, and it's for their own good. Children need to know what they can and can't do. Sometimes shouting or a telling off can be worse, especially if it's done in a way that makes the child look small or stupid. Too much criticism from parents can damage a child for life.

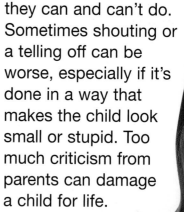

Sally: I've never smacked my children, although I've sometimes felt like it. If I did smack them it would be because of how I was feeling and not because of what they'd done.

Any parent knows that when you are feeling well, you don't mind if the children jump on the sofa. But you do when you are tired. What is a small child supposed to think if he gets smacked one day and ignored on another for exactly the same thing? What does smacking teach a child?

What do you do if you smack your child and they carry on? Smack them harder?

When my children misbehave, I refuse them treats. I send them out of the room. I shout at them. I don't smack my kids because I couldn't bear hurting them.

▶ Should children have the same right as adults not to be hit?

❓ Questions

1 Most people would agree that punishments should be fair, but what is a fair punishment? What makes a punishment unfair?

2 What are the arguments in favour of parents smacking or hitting their children? What are the arguments against this?

3 What do you feel is right?

Research

A government survey showed that more than nine out of every ten children had been physically punished and that three quarters of them were hit before they were a year old. Just over a quarter of seven-year-olds were hit more than once a week.

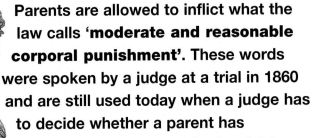

The law

Parents are allowed to inflict what the law calls 'moderate and reasonable corporal punishment'. These words were spoken by a judge at a trial in 1860 and are still used today when a judge has to decide whether a parent has unreasonably punished a child.

If the punishment causes the child unnecessary suffering or injury, or is inhuman or degrading, the parent may be committing an offence.

Punishment

Time for a change?

In the past

It wasn't until 1889 that children in England and Wales had any kind of special protection in law. In fact, laws banning cruelty to animals appeared some time before those preventing cruelty to children.

One reason for this was that many people believed the law should not interfere in private family life. Another was the difficulty of prosecuting a violent parent, as the law did not allow one member of a family to give evidence in court against another.

Today

Although **corporal punishment** is not allowed in schools or prisons, it is still part of many children's lives in Britain. All the main political parties are in favour of keeping the right of parents to smack their children.

Eight European countries – Austria, Croatia, Cyprus, Denmark, Finland, Latvia, Norway and Sweden – have made it an offence for a parent to hit a child. But parents are prosecuted only in very serious cases. Although they still do hit their children, it is thought to happen much less often than in the past. Most other countries do not forbid parents from hitting their children.

> This Government believes in parental discipline. Smacking has a place in that. Our law will do nothing to outlaw smacking.
>
> **Paul Boateng, Labour Minister for Health, 1999**

> I think there is much value in corporal punishment.
>
> **Gillian Shephard, when Conservative Secretary of State for Education**

Hitting out

When the head teacher at Adam's school learnt that Adam, aged 9, was being hit by his stepfather he got in touch with the social services. An investigation took place and Adam's stepfather was charged with assault.

In court, Adam's mother said that she hadn't known that her husband had been hitting Adam, but added that her son could be difficult to deal with. 'My son has been a handful since he was two,' she said. 'If I tell him off, he just looks through me.'

Adam's stepfather said that he had hit Adam with a metre-long garden

cane after the boy had misbehaved at school. He had also hit him when he had threatened his younger brother with a knife. Adam said that his stepfather had given him the stick more than once. 'I can't remember how many times,' he said in court. 'Sometimes he hit my legs. It hurt a lot when he did this.'

The judge explained to the **jury** that, in law, a parent was allowed to hit a child, even with a stick, if it was done 'moderately' and as a way of correcting a child's bad behaviour.

THINK! Do you think Adam's stepfather broke the law? Do you think the jury should find him guilty or not guilty?

The next stage

The jury decided that Adam's stepfather was not guilty of assault. But the case did not end there. In 1998, with support from his birth father, Adam's case was taken to the **European Court of Human Rights**.

The law in England and Wales allowed parents to use reasonable force to punish their children. However, the lawyers acting on Adam's behalf said that this let parents go too far in disciplining their children. They said that children needed greater protection and that the law should be changed.

The judges agreed. They decided that the law in England and Wales broke Article 3 of the European Convention on Human Rights, and told the British Government that it must change the law.

The European Convention on Human Rights Article 3: No one shall be subjected to torture or to inhuman or degrading treatment or punishment.

? Questions

1 What would be the advantages of a law making it an offence for a parent to hit their child, as it is in some other European countries? What would be the disadvantages?

2 What would you advise the Government to do?

Key Words

Corporal punishment
Physical punishment, such as caning or striking someone with a hand.

European Court of Human Rights
Anyone who feels that the law in this country has not dealt fairly with their rights can take their case to the European Court of Human Rights in Strasbourg.

Jury
A jury is made up of 12 people, aged 18–70, who have the job of listening to the evidence in a trial and deciding whether the person accused is guilty or not guilty.

Rights and responsibilities

In this unit we look at the ways in which our rights and responsibilities change as we get older.

When we get older

If someone asked you 'When do you become an adult?', what would you say? It's difficult to give a simple answer because, as far as the law is concerned, the change from being a child to an adult is very gradual.

? Questions

At what age does the law allow a person to do the following?

1 Buy cigarettes

2 Drive a car on the road

3 Vote in an election

4 Drink alcohol in a pub

5 Buy fireworks

6 Have sex with someone of the opposite sex

7 Buy a pet

8 Have a tattoo

9 Serve on a jury

10 Be convicted of a criminal offence

11 Give blood

12 See your school records

BIG BEN BONG

NATIONAL BLOOD SERVICE

Ready or not?

Marriage

In England and Wales you can marry at 16 with your parents' agreement (otherwise it's 18). In Scotland you can also marry at 16, but do not need permission from your parents. In France, girls can marry at 15, but boys must be 18. In Greece, the ages are 14 for girls and 18 for boys, but in Austria, they are 16 and 19. In Norway there is no minimum age for marriage but young people who want to marry before they are 18 need their parents' or local governor's permission.

> **THINK!** Why do you think some countries might allow girls to marry before boys? Is this a good idea? Should we do the same in Britain?

WANTED: BABY-FACE SMITH. FOR CRIMES AGAINST HIS NAPPY.

Crime

Young people in England and Wales become responsible for the crimes they commit when they are 10. In Scotland, it is 8. In France, it is 13 and in Norway it is 15. But young people in Belgium are not fully responsible for their crimes until they are 18.

> **THINK!** How do you decide at what age people should be responsible for their crimes?

Politics

In most countries, including Britain, people cannot vote until they are 18. Until 1969, the age limit was 21. When William Hague spoke at the Conservative Party Conference in 1977, he was still at school and only 16 years of age. Although he was able to tell Conservative politicians what he thought they ought to be doing, it was another two years before he was old enough to vote.

Some children know more about politics than their parents. They are of course also citizens, like everyone else. At 16, a young person may work full-time, pay taxes, get married and have sex. If they are old enough to do all this should they not have the right to vote for the political party that is to govern them?

> **THINK!** Do you think young people are ready to vote before they are 18?
>
> What difference do you think it would make if young people had the right to vote?

> **? Question**
>
> 1 Do you favour a single age at which you move from a child to an adult? If you do, what would it be? or, perhaps you would prefer to leave things as they are? Try to give a reason for your answer.

The ageing process

Alcohol and bars

It is against the law for a child below the **age of 5** to be given alcohol, except for medical reasons.

You can go into a pub alone at **14**, but only for soft drinks, and with the agreement of the landlord. If the pub has children's certificate, the landlord may allow you into the bar if you are under 14, but you must be with an adult and leave by 9pm.

From the **age of 16** you can have beer, cider or perry with a meal in a restaurant or a room used for meals in a pub or hotel. You can also buy liqueur chocolates.

You can buy alcohol in a pub or off-licence from the **age of 18**.

Animals

You can buy a pet from the **age of 12**.

Crime

You can give evidence in court at **any age**, as long as the court believes you understand the duty to tell the truth.

You are legally responsible for any crimes you commit from the **age of 10** and may be punished by a court.

From the **age of 18** you may serve on a jury.

Health

You can agree to, or refuse to have, medical treatment at **any age**, as long as the doctor or dentist feels that you understand the consequences of your decision.

You have a right, at **any age**, to see your health records as long as the doctor believes that you understand what you are looking for and that neither you nor anyone else will suffer serious harm from anything that you read.

You may give blood from the **age of 17** onwards.

Home

Your parents have responsibility for you and you are under their care until you are **18**. This means that, strictly speaking, you cannot leave home without their permission until then. However, the police rarely order sixteen- or seventeen-year-olds home unless they are in danger or are unable to look after themselves.

Leisure

You can see a U or PG film by yourself from the **age of 5** and a Category 15 film from the **age of 15**.

You can buy fireworks, place a bet and have a tattoo at **18**. Lottery tickets should not be sold to anyone **under 16**, nor can winnings be collected by anyone below this age.

Marriage

You can marry, with your parents' agreement, from the **age of 16**. If they won't agree, you have to wait until you are 18. Anyone who marries at 16 or 17 without their parents' permission is committing a crime – but their marriage is still valid (that is, legal).

Money and property

You can open a bank account at **any age** if the bank thinks you understand what is involved. But you won't be able to borrow money until you are **18**.

You cannot legally own land until you are **18** but you can inherit money or goods left in somebody's will.

Politics

You can vote in local, national and European elections when you are **18**.

You may become a local councillor or a Member of Parliament, the Welsh Assembly or the European Parliament from the **age of 21**.

School

From the **age of 5** you must receive full-time education, either at school or elsewhere.

You can ask to see your school records at **any age**, as long as the head teacher is satisfied that you want to see them for a genuine reason and that neither you nor anyone else will be harmed by what you read.

You can leave school on the last Friday in June of the school year in which you are **16**.

Sex

You have the right to receive confidential contraceptive treatment at **any age**, as long as the doctor or nurse believes that you understand what is involved.

A girl can agree to a man having sexual intercourse with her when she is **16**.

A man may agree to have sexual relations with another man in private, as long as he and his partner are **16 or over**. There is no lower age limit for sexual relations between women. But a woman aged 16 or over could be charged with indecent assault, or other sex offences, if her partner is under 16.

Tobacco

You can buy cigarettes, tobacco and cigarette papers from the **age of 16**. It is not an offence to smoke below this age, but uniformed police officers and park keepers do have the power to confiscate cigarettes from children under 16.

Travel

You can apply for your own passport when you are **16**, but will need your parents' written permission until you are **18**.

You have to pay a child's fare on most buses and trains from the **age of 5**, and full fare from **16**.

You can ride a moped up to 50cc when you are **16**, and a larger motorcycle, car or van at **17**. The age limit for driving a large van or lorry is **18** or **21**, depending on the weight of the vehicle.

From the **age of 14** you are responsible for wearing a seat belt in a car.

You can apply for a helicopter pilot's licence and hold a pilot's licence at **17**.

Work

You can work part-time from **13**, but the exact rules for this vary from one part of the country to another.

You must be at least **14** to work on a market – and even then you will need a licence or to be working for your parents.

You can join the armed forces from the age of **16** if your parents agree. If not, you must wait until you are **18**.

? Questions

Do any of the ages surprise you? Are there any that you think are unfair or should be changed? Are there any that you would abolish altogether?

diag**n**osis

symptoms

Too young to decide?

At 15, Melanie was just like many young people of her age. She was fit and active, and enjoyed netball and swimming. She also believed that she was perfectly healthy and that it would be many years before she would be troubled by illnesses that normally affect people much older than herself.

In May, however, Melanie suddenly became seriously ill with heart failure. So ill, in fact, the doctors said that, without a new heart, she would have just a few days to live. They explained to Melanie and her mum what a heart transplant operation would involve. They told Melanie that once she was over the operation, she would feel much stronger and could eventually lead quite a normal life. However, they said there would be some difficulties. There would be many visits to the hospital and, for the rest of her life, Melanie would be have to take 20 or 30 tablets a day.

If the right heart could be found, there was a good chance that Melanie would survive, but the doctors said that some of the drugs she would have to take could have painful and unpleasant side effects.

Melanie said that although she didn't want to die, she just couldn't face the rest of her life on drugs. She said that she would feel different from everyone else and added, 'I would rather die than have someone else's heart.'

decision

After a few days, the doctors found a heart that matched Melanie's weight, size and blood group. They carried out the operation – and Melanie survived.

The law

A young person can agree to receive medical treatment, as long as the doctor believes that they understand the effects of their decision.

If their parents were to object to this, a court would generally accept the young person's wishes, especially if their health was likely to be damaged by not having the treatment.

If a young person refuses treatment, a court has to decide whether they really understand the consequences of this.

If the judge believes that they do, then the child's wishes will normally be respected. But if the judge decides that the child is confused and not able to think about the issue properly, the judge can order that the operation or treatment goes ahead.

Although Melanie's mum said that the operation could go ahead, doctors did not want to begin unless Melanie also agreed. It was, after all, her life. They chose to go to court to ask a judge to decide.

> **(!) THINK!** Do you think the judge should tell the doctors to go ahead with the operation, even though it is not what Melanie wants?

The judge said that he felt that Melanie's illness had come so quickly that she hadn't really had a chance to think about everything properly. He thought that she was confused and worried and couldn't come to a proper decision. He told the doctors that they could go ahead with the operation. Melanie accepted what the judge had said.

(?) Questions

1 Do you think the judge was right to allow the doctors to go ahead with the operation?

2 What difference does it make to your answer if Melanie had died?

3 Is 15 old enough to know your own mind on a question of this sort?

Bullying

In this unit we ask why bullying takes place in schools and what can be done to deal with it.

Jessica's tale

'School's all right – well, most of it. I've got some good friends, although it's a pity they live so far away. I keep up with the work and I've just been picked for the school cross-country team. At the parents' evening, the teachers told my mum and dad that everything was going well. Which is nice. The only trouble is, that it isn't. My problem is the school bus. Not the bus itself, but some of the people on it.

'When the bus comes in the morning, it's always empty – apart from a boy in the sixth form who gets on at the stop before. At the next village, ten more people are picked up. They're all from my school. Most of them are older than me, but there's two or three from the year below.

'As soon as they got on the bus one morning, I knew they were talking about me. I've got ginger hair, which is long and frizzy and someone called me "crinkle cut". At first I tried to ignore it but it carried on for the rest of the journey with more people joining in. The next day it was the same, and the day after that. I tried moving to another seat, but it didn't do any good. In fact it got worse. If I shouted or told them to get lost, they just laughed at the way I spoke. I tried to block them out by reading a book or putting on my Walkman, but they still made fun of me.

'One day, one of the girls ran her hand through my hair as she got off the bus. It wasn't long before her friends were doing the same.

'The only time I don't get any bother is when the bus is full. Then I can hide amongst the crowd. It's been going on for nearly a term. I don't know what to do. I have to use the bus to get to school, but all my friends travel on other routes, so there's no one to talk to or to stick up for me. I can't tell anyone about it. I feel so stupid.'

1 How do you think Jessica is feeling? Why do you think she can't tell anyone she is being bullied?

2 Who do you think is responsible for her difficulties?

3 What do you think Jessica should do?

4 Try to describe the different kinds of hurt felt by people who are bullied.

Rubber Legs

Here is an advert that appeared in a local newspaper:

It's Rubber Legs Roberts!

Did you go to school with 'Peter Rubber Legs Roberts' who in 1953 at the age of 15 was a pupil at Rossington Secondary Modern School? Can anyone remember bullying Peter at school? If so, he would like to invite you to spend a weekend on his yacht and discuss your problem. Peter bears no ill will to all his old school chums and sends them his best wishes and hopes you are all keeping well.

THINK! Why do you think Peter Roberts placed this advertisement?

The law

Schools have a legal duty to make sure that children are safe while they are in school – which includes their journey to and from school on the school bus. This means that teachers and governors should do their best to stop pupils from bullying one another. All schools should have a policy on how they deal with bullying. They must try to do something about the situation as soon as they know that bullying is taking place.

Bullying

In this unit we ask why bullying takes place and what can be done to deal with it.

Rights and wrongs

What is bullying?

A bully is someone who uses their power to frighten or hurt someone else. Bullying can take many forms. Sometimes it is *physical* – when the person is deliberately hurt or has something taken away from them. Often bullying involves *mental cruelty* – calling someone names, or making them look and feel very stupid.

People often think that bullying happens only in school. In fact it takes place in many situations, particularly at work and in the home. It's a problem that affects adults as well as children.

Who does it happen to?

Studies over the last ten years show that between a quarter and a third of boys and girls say that they are bullied in some way at school. More girls than boys believe that they are bullied.

Anyone can be bullied. We're probably less likely to be bullied when we are feeling happy and good about ourselves. It's the times when we don't feel so clever or fit or healthy that we are likely to be picked upon.

The same can be true for the people who do the bullying – which can also be us, or our friends. Bullies also have a problem with their confidence or their feelings. If we are angry or jealous or uncertain about ourselves, we sometimes try to put other people down, so that we can look better.

How does it make people feel?

Bullying hurts. It makes us feel upset and scared. Sometimes it can be terrifying. We don't know what to do or how to stop it. We skip school. We worry and try to avoid seeing certain people. It can make our life a hell and make us feel totally inadequate.

In serious cases there can come a point where people feel that they cannot face it any more and, tragically, they take their own life.

What should we do?

All the experts agree that anyone who is being bullied should tell someone they can trust what has been happening. This can be a parent, friend or teacher, and it should be done as soon as possible.

Some schools have peer mediators, who are pupils trained to listen and help with problems like bullying. Sometimes they can be very effective in helping to sort out such difficulties.

If the bullying is connected with school, it's important to talk to a teacher you can trust. Although the difficulties may seem huge, teachers and parents together can do a great deal to help by approaching the problem in the right way. They don't have to take over. You have a right to be involved in what you would like to happen.

If you see someone being bullied, there are several things you can do. Probably the *worst* thing is either to ignore it or to go along with the bullying. The *best* thing is to provide the person with some sort of support or friendship and to explain to a teacher, or another adult, what has been happening.

Bullying – a criminal offence

Teachers called in the police after a serious outbreak of bullying at a school in Doncaster, South Yorkshire. Over a period of several months, ten boys, aged between 13 and 15, threatened and robbed other pupils of their dinner money and bus fares.

The boys were arrested after an early morning raid by police at their homes, and were later charged with a range of offences including blackmail, threatening behaviour and robbery. All were found guilty. Three of the boys were sent to a young offender institution and the remaining seven were fined or sent to an attendance centre and ordered to pay their victims compensation.

❓ Questions

1 How do you think schools and teachers should deal with bullying?

2 Do you think the head teacher of the school in Doncaster was right to call the police? Why don't schools do this more often? When should the police be involved?

3 How should schools treat people who bully?

Key Words

Attendance Centre
A Saturday afternoon centre, normally run by the police or prison officers for young offenders.

Blackmail
Trying to obtain money or putting pressure on someone unfairly by threatening to cause them some kind of harm.

Young offender institution
This is the equivalent of a prison for young people, between the ages of 15 and 21.

Right and wrong

In this unit we ask who should be responsible when young people break the law and at what age they should be held responsible for their crimes.

Growing up

This is Joel – he's ten months old.

At two-weeks-old he already showed signs of being able to tell the difference between certain kinds of sound. When he heard his mum or dad talking softly he reacted with pleasure. If he heard them raise their voice to Jessica, his seven-year-old sister, he usually cried.

By the time Joel was three-months-old, he recognised his mum or dad by sight. At six months he was able to sit up by himself and when he is a year old he may just be able to walk. When he is three, he will go to nursery school and when he is five, he will be in school every day.

THINK!
When do you think Joel will understand the difference between right and wrong?

How will Joel learn that some things are right, and others are wrong?

Taking responsibility

As he grows older, like everybody else, Joel will probably break the law. He will eventually be old enough to take responsibility for this, in law.
This is called the **age of criminal responsibility**. As you can see from the examples below, this varies a great deal from one country to another.

Age of criminal responsibility	
Cyprus, Ireland, Switzerland	7
Scotland	8
England and Wales	10
France	13
Austria, Germany, Italy	14
Denmark, Norway, Sweden	15
Portugal, Spain	16
Belgium, Luxembourg	18

Parents

In Britain, parents are not normally held responsible for their children's crimes, unless it can be shown that they gave their child practical help or encouragement.

However, they are responsible for paying their child's court fines if he or she is under 16, and they can be ordered to pay up to £5,000 compensation to the victim.

Parents can be ordered by courts to attend special guidance sessions to learn how to stop their children from getting into any more serious trouble. Parents who ignore this can be put on **probation** or fined up to £1,000,

 In France, parents can be fined and sent to prison for up to two years, for failing to discipline their children. Madame Ignalzak had four sons, aged 12 to 17, who committed so many crimes that the court decided to jail her for a month. 'I can't supervise them 24 hours a day,' she told the court. 'I go to sleep, and the boys go out the window.'

Gareth

Gareth's name and picture were often in the news. When he was 11, he was filmed by a TV crew, driving a stolen car. He was in the papers again at the age of 18, when he died – almost certainly from a drugs overdose.

Gareth lived in a house on a pleasant housing estate in a town in County Durham. He belonged to a close family, but several of his relatives, including his dad and elder brother, had criminal records. At 11 he was excluded from school for bad attendance, and it was from this time that his crimes became very serious. By the time of his death, he had 40 **convictions**, mostly for theft. He had missed so much school that he could barely read or write.

The law

Children must be 10, or over, to be arrested or charged with a crime. But, in cases of very serious misbehaviour, a court can order a child under 10 to stay at home during certain hours.

? Questions ??

1 Why do you think children like Gareth become involved in crime at such a young age?

2 Madame Ignalzak says she can't supervise the children all day? How fair is it to blame parents for their children's actions?

3 What do you think the age of criminal responsibility should be in this country? Why do you think it should be this age?

Key Words

Age of criminal responsibility
The age at which a person becomes responsible in law for a crime and can be punished by a court.

Conviction
When a court finds a person guilty of a crime

Probation
A sentence given out by a court, requiring a person to behave well and keep out of trouble for anything between six months and three years. Anyone on probation who commits another offence in this time can be sentenced for both the new and the original offences.

Crime

In this unit we look at some of the ways in which courts decide whether a person is responsible for a crime.

All in the mind?

 THINK! Look carefully at the picture. What do the boys seem to be doing? Is there any evidence that they are breaking the law? What would you need to know to help you decide whether a crime is being committed?

The law

Taking a bicycle: It is an offence to take a bicycle, without the owner's permission, for your own, or someone else's use. Strictly speaking, it's even an offence just to ride a bike without the owner's permission.

Theft: A person is guilty of theft if it is shown that they dishonestly took something that belonged to someone else with the intention of either not giving it back or keeping it permanently.

Criminal damage: It is an offence deliberately to destroy or damage, without a good reason, something that belongs to someone else.

Criminal responsibility: The age of criminal responsibilty is 10. Children under 10 are treated in law as being too young to decide what is right and wrong.

Guilty or not guilty? Although the law can be very complicated, there are normally two things that must be shown before a person is convicted of a crime. The first is that an offence has been committed, for example, that something has been taken or damaged, or that someone has been hurt. Secondly, it must normally be shown that the person accused intended to do what they did, or did not care about the consequences of their actions. However there are some offences, like speeding, for which a person is automatically guilty – even if they were not intending to go fast or didn't realise they were breaking the law.

No excuse

About 1000 years ago, when a system of law was first being set up in England, courts judged the people accused on what they had done – and not on what they had intended to do. It made no difference, for example, whether you injured someone accidentally or on purpose. You were simply judged on the damage that you had caused. It was only in the thirteenth century, under the influence of the Church, that courts started to look at the intention of a person in deciding their guilt.

? Questions

Is it a crime? Look at the following cases and decide whether you think a crime has taken place. Try to explain the reasons for your answer.

1   Mark pays for his groceries without noticing that his 4-year-old daughter has helped herself to a bar of chocolate at the checkout. Mark only sees the chocolate in the little girl's hand after they have left the shop.

2   Sara's mother gives her £5 to buy some blank videos. Sara takes a pack of three tapes from a display stand in a store without paying for them and keeps the money her mother gave her. No one in the store realises that the tapes have been stolen.

3   Luke is a waiter in a restaurant. A couple come in for an early evening meal. The retaurant is still empty when they leave. As he is clearing the table Luke sees that the woman has left her handbag. He picks it up, checks that no one else is in the room, opens the bag and searches for money or anything else of value. He finds nothing and puts the bag back down on the floor.

Who's to blame?

Shipwreck!

On 19 May 1884, four men set sail to Australia from Southampton in a yacht called the *Mignonette*. On 5 July, in the middle of the south Atlantic Ocean, a storm arose and the boat was hit by a huge wave. It quickly started to sink. The men had time to grab only two tins of turnips before they climbed into a small open boat. Soon afterwards, the *Mignonette* went down.

After three days, the men managed to catch a small turtle but nine days later, this and the few turnips had all gone. They were 1000 miles from land, with no food and just the occasional drop of water to drink.

 What do you think the men could do?

There was, however, one chance of survival – at least for three of the crew. The Captain, Thomas Dudley, suggested that one of them could be sacrificed to feed the others. The men objected. 'If we are to die,' they said, 'we should all die together.'

Two days later, they were still without food and water and the youngest member of the crew, Richard Parker, lay almost unconscious at the bottom of the boat. In an effort to quench his thirst he had begun to drink sea water.

The Captain again suggested that one of them should be sacrificed.

 What should the men decide? How should they reach a decision? What should happen if they cannot agree?

As they talked over the problem it seemed that Richard was the obvious choice. He was 17 years old. He had no wife or family and he was already on the edge of death. The three men agreed that, if no help came by the next day, Richard Parker would have to die. What they couldn't agree, however, was who would do the deed. Seaman Brooks said he wanted no part in the killing.

And so, with his knife, the Captain slit the throat of the unconscious boy. In case there was a struggle, first mate Edwin Stephens stood ready to hold down Richard's feet.

Over the next three days, all three men drank the blood and ate the heart and liver of the unfortunate boy. On the fourth day, they were spotted by a ship that stopped to pick them up.

The journey back to England took about six weeks. As soon as they reached Falmouth in Cornwall, the Captain went straight to the police to explain what had happened.

> **(!) THINK!** What should the Captain say to the police? Do you think a crime has been committed? If so, by whom?

The Captain told the police that Richard Parker had died and explained how it had happened. Shortly afterwards he and Edwin Stephens were arrested and charged with murder. No charges were brought against Seaman Brooks.

> **(!) THINK!** Do you think the Captain and Stephens should be found guilty of murder? What points would you put forward to make your case?

> **(!) THINK!** How much responsibility did Seaman Brooks have for what happened? Was he equally to blame?

The trial

Captain Thomas Dudley and Edwin Stephens were both found guilty. At that time, anyone found guilty of murder would normally have been executed. However, because of the unusual circumstances the men eventually received a pardon from the Queen and served six months in prison.

The law

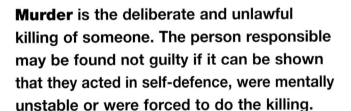

Murder is the deliberate and unlawful killing of someone. The person responsible may be found not guilty if it can be shown that they acted in self-defence, were mentally unstable or were forced to do the killing.

Cannibalism, the eating of dead human flesh, is not against the law.

In law, anyone who helps someone commit a crime is normally guilty of the same crime themselves. For example, the person who acts as a look-out or drives the getaway car in a robbery would be charged with the same offence as the man or woman who held the bank cashier at gunpoint.

Crime

What's the charge?

An accomplice to the crime

We saw in the last section that anyone who helps or encourages a person to commit an offence can be arrested and charged with that offence, just like the main offender.

? Questions

Look at the cases below. Decide who you think would be charged with an offence and what that offence might be.

Case 1: Danny takes a shirt from a rack, intending to steal it. He asks his friend Paul to hide the shirt in his bag and give it to him outside the shop.

Case 2: Michelle tells Billy that a large amount of money is always kept in the office where she works. She tells Billy that she doesn't want any of the money, but gives him the code that switches off the burglar alarm.

Case 3: Terry and Wayne plan to rob a man in the street. Wayne pushes him over and Terry grabs the man's case. As the man falls, he bangs his head and later dies in hospital.

Case 4: As Nazali walks down the street, a car pulls up beside her. It's Simon. 'Jump in,' he shouts. 'Let's go for a drive.' Nazali gets in beside him, knowing that the car is almost certainly stolen.

Case 5: Ben and Carl plan to break into a house and Ben gives Carl a knife in case they need to defend themselves. Inside the house, the owner hears them and comes downstairs to investigate. Ben shouts 'Let's go', jumps out of the window and runs away. But Carl stabs the man and kills him.

Chain gang

Laura had never really wanted to do this kind of thing, but she had now done it twice. Four or five of them go into a shop. One person asks for something behind the counter and, while the assistant is not looking, the others just help themselves. Then they leave as soon as possible. The trouble is, how do you stop?

? Questions ? ? ? ? ? ?

1 What is Laura's problem?

2 What risks is she taking?

3 Why do you think she is finding the situation so difficult?

4 What choices are open to Laura? Which should she choose?

The Gunpowder Plot

Th Gunpowder Plot is an early example of action taken by the law (at the time) when a group of people planned a crime together. James I became King of England in 1603. Soon after his coronation, he ordered all Catholic priests to leave the country and announced that anyone who did not go to church – the Protestant Church, that is – would be fined.

Catholics were in a very difficult position. If they attended their own secret church services, they risked imprisonment or death. If they refused to go to church, they were fined. It made them very angry. They wanted to have the right to worship freely.

In 1605 a small group of Catholics decided to try to do something about this. They plotted to kill the King by blowing him up – along with all the MPs, bishops and lords.

The occasion was going to be the state opening of Parliament, which was due to take place on 5 November. On the night of 4 November, however, the Government received an anonymous warning. A man called Guy Fawkes was arrested as he guarded the explosives that the plotters were going to use, directly underneath the Houses of Parliament.

Although Fawkes was not one of the ringleaders, he was tortured by the King's soldiers to try to make him name the others involved in the plot. Eventually he gave in. The men were rounded up, put on trial for treason, and executed.

They had all broken the law in planning to kill the King. It made no difference what part they had played. In the eyes of the law, all those involved were guilty of treason.

Racism

In this unit we look at the responsibility that people have to deal with racist crimes.

Nothing's easy

Vicki was 16 and had been going out with Mark for about a month. She had met him at a club and they were seeing each other three or four times a week.

Mark was nearly 20. He worked in a bank. He had lots of friends and Vicki enjoyed being with him.

One evening, they had a slight disagreement. Vicki was tired. She left Mark with his friends and decided to walk home alone. After she got back from school the following day, Mark rang to see how she was. Vicki said she was all right and asked him what he'd been doing.

'I've been in a fight,' Mark said. 'What happened?' asked Vicki, worried that he had been hurt. 'We had a go at this bloke,' Mark explained. Vicki thought he sounded pleased. 'We gave him such a kicking.'
'How did it start?', asked Vicki.
'They had no right to be in the pub,' said Mark. 'I don't think they'll come back.

We'll be OK. The police don't know it was us.'

Vicki didn't know what to think. Had Mark actually enjoyed beating up this poor man? She said that her tea was ready, and rang off.

Later in the evening Vicki saw the local news on television. Rajeev, a young Asian man, had been seriously assaulted the night before. He, and two others, had been out for a drink. They were on their way home when they were attacked by a gang of about ten white youths. They showed his picture on the screen. Rajeev's head was so swollen that it was difficult to make out the shape of his eyes, nose and ears.

The telephone rang again. It was Mark. 'Did you see it on television? That was us. We did that.' Vicki quietly put down the receiver.

 What do you think Vicki should do?

Vicki went upstairs to her room. An hour later she came down again and told her Mum everything she knew. At midnight she telephoned the police.

The next day Mark was arrested. In his bedroom the police found a pair of shoes on which were found traces of blood, belonging to Rajeev's blood group.

It was not long before people knew that Vicki had given Mark's name to the police. In the eight months before Mark's trial, Vicki received many threats. She had anonymous phone calls and was bullied at school. Someone twice threatened to cover her with petrol and set light to it. Not even Vicki's dog was spared – it was fed meat spiked with glass. Many people believed that Vicki had been wrong to go to the police.

THINK! **What do you think Vicki should have done? Was she right to go to the police?**

Would it have been wrong if she had *not* gone to the police?

Mark refused to tell the police who else took part in the attack. Local people knew the names of the other members of the group, but no one was prepared to tell the police.

Rajeev lay in a coma for several weeks, and his face remains permanently damaged. Mark was sentenced to 12 months' imprisonment.

The law

It is a serious offence to assault someone causing **grievous bodily harm.** The maximum punishment for this is life imprisonment. Courts can increase the punishment for less serious crimes if the victim has been chosen because of their race, colour or ethnic background.

It is against the law to lie to the police or to prevent them from making their enquiries, but there is no law saying that people have to tell the police if they believe that someone they know has committed a crime.

? Questions

1 How would you decide whether to give the police the name of a friend or member of your family whom you believe has been involved in a crime?

2 Some people believe that racist attacks should be treated more seriously than other forms of violence. Do you agree? Try to explain your answer.

Key Words

Grievous bodily harm
Causing someone serious injury or harm.

Racism

Racist crime

Men are much more likely to commit racist offences than women.

Sadly, people can become victims of crime just because of the colour of their skin or where they, or their relatives, have originally come from.

It is impossible to know exactly how often this happens. Not all crimes are reported to the police and it can be very difficult to decide why a particular crime took place. It could be because of the colour of the victim's skin, but it is often hard to know.

Peace at last

Marcia and her 10-year-old son were not the only black people on their estate. For some reason, however, they faced continuous trouble from one particular group of boys. At first Marcia tried to ignore it. When this didn't work, she spoke to the boys and, finally, called round to see their parents. Eventually she complained to the council who investigated the situation and took the parents of one of the boys to court. The court ordered the boy's parents to leave their house, which they rented from the council. The parents appealed against this, saying that the cause of the problem was not their behaviour, but that of their son. The judge disagreed. He said that Marcia and her son should not be deprived of their rights just because the parents could not control their son.

A picture of Britain today

There are, however, certain things that we do know about racist crime.

- Racist crime affects people of all colours and nationalities.

- The number of racist crimes that are reported to the police has increased greatly in recent years. It is not clear whether this is because there is more crime, or because people are now more prepared to come forward and tell the police about racist incidents.

- Black and Asian people are much more likely to be victims of racist crime than white people, but white people suffer from racist crime as well.

The law

Everyone knows that robbery and violence are against the law. But if the victim has been chosen because of their race, colour or ethnic background, courts have the power to increase the punishment given. It is an offence to use racist language in public in a way that is designed to harass or alarm someone. It's also against the law to put up abusive signs or posters.

Anyone who racially harasses their neighbour can be **prosecuted** by their local council. If the person responsible lives in a council house, the council can make them leave their home.

? Questions ? ? ? ? ?

1 Think about the ways in which racist behaviour shows itself and how people's lives are affected by it.

2 What do you think people should do when they hear or see racist behaviour?

Key Words

Prosecute
To bring a criminal case against someone to court.

The case of Stephen Lawrence

Stephen Lawrence was a young man of 18, living in Plumstead in south-east London. On 22 April 1993, at about 10.30pm, he was waiting to catch a bus home with his friend Duwayne. Checking to see if there was any sign of a bus coming, Stephen walked a little way back down the road. He was seen by a group of five young white men on the other side of the road. They quickly crossed over and surrounded Stephen, who was standing alone. Stephen was stabbed on both sides of his body – in his chest and in his arm.

The five people who had attacked Stephen immediately ran away.

As soon as Duwayne realised that he and his friend were in danger, he shouted to Stephen and told him to run. Somehow Stephen managed to get to his feet, and both young men crossed the road in the direction of their home. However, Stephen was seriously injured and, after struggling about 100 metres, he collapsed on the pavement, where he died.

The events of that night are remembered, not only because of this tragic attack, but also because of the slowness and inefficiency of the police in trying to find those responsible. No one has yet been arrested or charged with Stephen's murder.

Working lives

In this unit we look at what the law says about children working and ask whether children are protected enough from the dangers involved.

Children's hours

No news today

Just before he was due to start his morning paper round, Wayne got a call from the newsagent, Mr Moss. 'You've been making too many mistakes,' said Mr Moss. 'I've told you before that the papers have to be pushed right through the letter box, not left sticking half way out. Don't bother coming in this morning, or any other morning. You're fired.'

Wayne, who was 15, didn't want to lose his job. He didn't think he had been treated fairly. 'I've worked for Mr Moss for two years. I don't think he has any right to sack me without a proper warning, especially for something so small,' he told his mum. 'He would never treat an adult like this.'

Wayne took his complaint to an employment tribunal, claiming that he had been unfairly dismissed. Mr Moss asked his solicitor what he should do, and she said that he should try to come to some agreement with Wayne, before the case reached the court. Mr Moss offered Wayne two weeks' wages (£18) as compensation, which Wayne accepted.

> **(!)** **THINK!** Do you think Wayne was fairly treated by Mr Moss?

Work force

There are probably about two million children in work in England and Wales at any one time. That's about one in three children aged between 10 and 16. Between a quarter and a third of the children who work have more than one job. Girls are slightly less likely to work than boys, although numbers are similar by the time they reach 15 or 16.

In 1999, a survey of children working on Tyneside in north-east England found that the most common jobs were paper rounds and leaflet delivery. The researchers talked to over 1000 children, in five schools. The list on the top of the page opposite shows the places where they discovered that most children were working.

Working wages

In June 2000 the National Minimum Wage for 18–21-year-olds was set at £3.20 per hour. In October 2000 the hourly rate for those aged 22 and over was set at £3.70 per hour.

Sometimes the pay that children receive is very low indeed. Some 13-year-olds earn 50p an hour, or less. Council officials in Staffordshire recently discovered that a 13-year-old boy, who cut the potatoes each day for the local fish and chip shop, was paid nothing at all. He just received a free

The places that children work the most

- **Door-to-door deliveries**
- **Supermarkets**
- **Newsagents**
- **Hairdressers**
- **Pubs**
- **Butchers**
- **Department stores**
- **Amusement arcades**
- **Farms**
- **Cafés and restaurants**
- **Homes for the elderly**
- **Offices**
- **Stables**
- **Factories**
- **At home**

The pay that children receive is usually less than half what an adult would earn doing the same job.

If you are under 18, your pay is set at the rate agreed between you and your employer. If you don't think your employer is offering you enough, you might decide not to take the job.

meal at the end of his shift. The Tyneside survey found that the average pay for boys and girls aged 10–16 was £2.24 per hour. Boys tended to earn less than girls.

| Boys, average hourly rate | £1.93 |
| Girls, average hourly rate | £2.75 |

The law

All workers are protected in law against unfair dismissal as long as they have worked for their employer for at least a year. It makes no difference whether they are part- or full-time workers.

THINK! How do these rates compare with the wages children earn where you live?

Questions

1 Why do you think children work? What benefits do you think they get out of working?

2 Look at the list of jobs that the researchers found children were doing. What do you think about the places where the children worked? Can you see any dangers or problems?

3 Should there be a minimum wage for children? If you think there should, what rate should that be?

Is it legal?

Special laws cover the kind of work that children are and are not allowed to do. By 'child' the law means anyone not yet old enough to leave school.

The laws controlling the employment of children are set by each local authority, so they vary from one area to another. They are known as **by-laws**.

You should be able to get a copy of the employment by-laws in your area from a senior teacher at school, the local careers office, the library or the educational welfare service.

Age

> SORRY MISS! I'VE GOT TO GET TO WORK!

You normally need to be at least 13-years-old to be able to work part-time. The only kind of work you can normally do when you are under 13 is light farm work, with the supervision of one of your parents.

Hours

If you are not yet old enough to leave school, the law says you are not allowed to work:
- before 7am or after 7pm
- during school hours
- for more than two hours on a school day
- for more than one hour before school starts
- for more than two hours on Sundays.

People under 15 may work for only four hours a day on Saturdays and in holiday times and for a maximum of 25 hours a week. People aged 15 or 16 may work up to eight hours on Saturdays and in school holidays and 35 hours a week.

Breaks

> BUT DAD I HAVE TO HAVE 2 WEEKS WHEN I DON'T DO ANY WORK!

If you work for more than four hours in a day, you must have a break of at least an hour and there must be two weeks in the year when you don't do any kind of work at all.

Type of work

If you are not old enough to leave school you probably will not be able to:
- deliver milk
- sell alcohol, cigarettes or medicines
- work in a butcher's shop or slaughterhouse
- work in a kitchen or chip shop

> ARE YOU SURE YOU'RE OLD ENOUGH TO WORK HERE?

- work in an amusement arcade or fairground
- work more than three metres above floor level

- use dangerous machinery or work in any kind of job that might cause you some harm or injury.

You may not work on a market until you are 14 and even then you will need either a special licence or to be working with a parent.

Permits

Whenever a child is employed, the employer must apply to the local authority for an employment permit. This should be done within one week of the child starting work. The permit may be refused if the job is not suitable or the child is not regularly attending school.

Many employers ignore these rules, but a child who works without a permit may not be insured against accidents.

> DO YOU HAVE TO GIVE HER A LICENCE?

Entertainment

You will almost certainly need an entertainment licence if you are being paid to take part in a sport, to act as a model or to perform in a show, play or concert. You should be able to get details from your school or local education office.

Employment

The law says that you are employed if you do any kind of work for a business or organisation that is carried on for profit. This includes helping one of your parents with their work and it makes no difference whether or not you are paid.

KeyWords

By-laws
The government gives local councils the power to make their own laws and rules. These are called by-laws, from the Danish word *by*, meaning town. They cover all kinds of situations, from working hours for children to where you can walk your dog.

Babysitting
Babysitting for friends and neighbours is not normally seen as employment, unless it becomes a regular childminding job after school. There is no law setting out the minimum age for babysitting, but if something went wrong, a court would probably decide that someone under 16 was not fit for the job, and the parents would be at fault for not making proper arrangements for their child to be cared for.

Children at work
Records show that until the start of the nineteenth century it was quite common for children and adults to work together. When the Industrial Revolution began to take place, many more people, including children, moved from employment on the land to work in mills, factories and mines. Working conditions were often terrible, particularly for children, who were sometimes employed to do the most dangerous of jobs.

Gradually, laws were passed removing children from the worst of these dangers by reducing their hours, stopping them from being employed in certain kinds of work – and making them go to school.

Getting it right

Accidents at work

It is very difficult to know exactly how many children are seriously injured at work each year, because officials believe that many of the accidents are not recorded. Tragically, each year a small number of children are killed at work. Jamie, aged 12, worked in his spare time on a farm close to where he lived in Lancashire. One of the jobs that he often did was to help the farmer look after the sheep. Jamie liked the work, particularly because he was able to use the farmer's all-terrain vehicle – a three-wheel motorcycle with very fat tyres.

No one knows exactly how Jamie died. He was found in a ditch alongside the field in which he had been working alone. He was lying in water underneath the vehicle, with serious injuries to his head and arm. When the police recovered the vehicle they discovered that the brakes were faulty and that the farmer had known about this for some time. They also found a notice fixed to the side saying that it should not be driven by anyone below the age of 14. The farmer, Mr Burton, was charged with allowing a child to use a farm vehicle. He pleaded guilty and was fined £2,750.

THINK! Mr Burton clearly broke the law in allowing Jamie to use the all-terrain vehicle. What do you feel about the punishment he received? Was it fair? Should anybody else share the responsibility for what happened?

Packet money

Alan Coley began his packaging business five years ago. He can pack almost anything, but it's mainly small items for the house – like elastic bands, paper clips, screws or electric fuses. A lot of his work is done for a large chain of supermarkets.

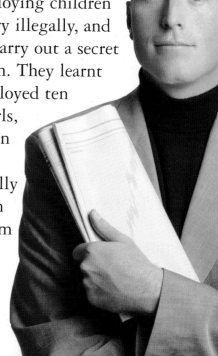
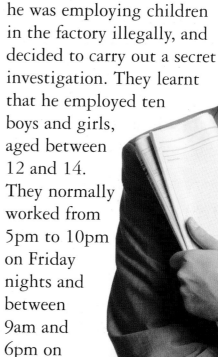

His local council heard that he was employing children in the factory illegally, and decided to carry out a secret investigation. They learnt that he employed ten boys and girls, aged between 12 and 14. They normally worked from 5pm to 10pm on Friday nights and between 9am and 6pm on

Saturdays. It was unusual for them to work on Sundays, unless Mr Coley had a major order. None of the children had an employment permit.

When Mr Coley realised that he was going to be prosecuted he was very angry.

'All I've done,' he said, 'is give these kids something to occupy their minds and give them a chance to earn a decent wage.

'If there were more people like me,' he went on, 'we wouldn't have them standing on street corners and getting into trouble.

'I can't see the harm in children working like this. How come nobody minds about kids delivering papers, getting up at six and going off on their own in the dark? That's what I call slave labour.'

Mr Coley was taken to court and fined. Afterwards the council solicitor said that it was impossible to prosecute all the employers who broke the law. He also thought the fines were so small that employers didn't take any notice.

? Questions

1 Was Mr Coley harming children or helping them, as he claimed?

2 Legally speaking, what had Mr Coley done wrong? Try to be as exact in your answer as you can.

3 Who was responsible for the law being broken? Was it Mr Coley alone, or should others also take responsibility?

4 What do you think the law should say about children at work? Do you think it should be changed?

A duty of care

In this unit we ask what should happen if something we buy is not as safe as it should be.

A snail's place

On the evening of 26 August 1928, May Donoghue and her friend walked into a small teashop in the town of Paisley, near Glasgow.

After they had sat down, Mr Minchella, the café owner, came over to ask what they would like. May's friend ordered pears and ice-cream for herself, and a ginger beer and ice-cream for May.

A few minutes later, Mr Minchella brought May's ice-cream and a dark glass bottle of Stevenson's ginger beer. He opened the bottle in front of May, and poured some of the fizzy drink over the ice-cream.

May took a drink, and her friend began to refill her glass. As she was pouring out the rest of the ginger beer, May saw what she believed were the remains of a snail!

The thought of what she had just drunk made May feel very ill. With bad stomach pains and gasro-enteritis, May went to her doctor and then to hospital at the Glasgow Royal Infirmary.

When May had recovered she sued David Stevenson, the maker of the ginger beer, for damages. She argued that it was Stevenson's job to make sure that snails did not get into the bottles of pop.

> **(!) THINK!** **What do you think are the most important points of this case?**
>
> **Does May have a reason to complain? Who do you think is in the wrong?**

It took May Donoghue four years to take her case through the courts. This was because, if she were to win, May would need a change in the law.

As things stood at the time, May had no case against Stevenson's, the makers of the ginger beer, because it was her friend, and not May, who had bought the drink.

The Law Lords decided that the makers of something, such as ginger beer, have a duty to make sure their products do not injure anyone who might use them. It should not, they said, make any difference whether the person concerned had or had not bought the item themself.

❓ Questions

1. Make a list of what you think are the most important points in the case of the snail in the bottle.

2. Look at the following cases and discuss what you think should happen. You need to decide whether the facts are similar to the case of the snail in the bottle. If they are, then you should come to the same decision as the judges in the case of Donoghue v Stevenson.

Darren bought a coffee and a hot fruit pie from a fast food restaurant. As he took his first bite of the pie, the fruit spurted out, burning his hand.

Kelly, aged 4, sat down and started to eat the fish fingers and beans that her dad, Brian, had just cooked. He was in the kitchen washing up when he heard his daughter coughing. She seemed to be choking, and nothing Brian could do would stop it. He decided that Kelly should go to hospital, where they removed a 2.5 cm piece of fish bone from her throat.

Ross bought a ham salad sandwich from the supermarket. He unwrapped the sandwich but, before eating it, decided to check that the ham did not contain too much fat. As he inspected the meat he discovered a piece of wire on the lettuce.

A duty of care

Trading standards

Accident or crime?

Benny, who was 20, was a passenger in the back of his friend's car. They were driving through Manchester at 50 mph in a 40 mph zone. The weather was wet. As they turned a corner, the car skidded and hit a tree. Both Benny and his friend were killed.

The police discovered two important points. The first was that there was very little tread on one of the car tyres. The second was that the car had split into two as it hit the tree. The police said it was this which almost certainly cost Benny his life.

The car in which Benny had been travelling was made up of two separate bodies – the front of one car, and the back of another. They had been cut up and welded together, but Benny's friend did not realise that this was the car that he had bought.

> **THINK!** Who do you think was responsible for Benny's death?

> ! **THINK!** What do you think the police should do once their investigation has been completed?

Benny's friend had a duty of care to drive safely and to make sure that his car was safe for other people to travel in. The person who sold it to him had a duty not to sell a dangerous product. 'A lovely runner' was the salesman's description of the car.

If you buy something that you think is dangerous, you can report the matter to your local trading standards office. Their number is in the phone book under the name of your local council. They have a duty to investigate the problem and can prosecute the person or company responsible.

They will also give you advice on how to get your money back or to obtain compensation for any damage caused by the faulty goods.

The law

Shops and garages must make sure that the goods they sell are safe. If they are not, they or the company who made them may be prosecuted.

? Questions

1 Look at each of the following cases. Work out what has been done wrong in each case, how serious this is and who you feel is responsible.

All sorts

A customer complained that the 'best before' date on a packet of liquorice she had bought from a mini market had been changed. The **trading standards department** investigated and found many other tins and packets of food in the shop that should no longer have been on sale. Some of these were more than a year out of date. The owner said that his wife normally carried out the checks, but that he didn't have any records of when this was last done.

Burning issue

Many people have died when furniture in their homes has caught fire and burnt very quickly. The owner of a second-hand furnishing store was charged with selling a three-piece suite, costing £60, containing foam and fillings that would not pass current fire regulations. The owner of the shop, Mr Cunningham, did not appear in court to hear the case against him.

Fishy business

Amrik telephoned his local trading standards office when he got an electric shock from the pump he had bought for his aquarium. Trading standards officers tested all the pumps on sale at the pet shop where Amrik had bought his, and told the owner, Mr Dickens, to have them repaired.

Soon afterwards, the officers received another call, saying that Mr Dickens was also selling fireworks to children under 18. They investigated this by sending a 15-year-old boy to the store, and he was able to buy some bangers and rockets. None of these passed British safety regulations.

The check on the fireworks also revealed that Mr Dickens still had the electric pumps for sale, and none of the repairs had been made.

Mr Dickens said that he had told his staff to take the pumps off the shelves but had not checked that this had been done. He said that the 4000 bangers and 1000 mini rockets were left over from stock he had bought two years earlier. He said he didn't know they were illegal.

2 Who do you think is responsible for making sure that the goods that people sell are not dangerous?

3 Should anyone be charged with an offence? If so, who should it be and for what offence?

KeyWords

Prosecute
To bring a criminal case against someone to court.

Trading standards department
An office, run by the local authority, which tries to make sure that shops, restaurants and businesses trade legally with members of the public. They are sometimes also known as consumer protection departments.

Driving lessons

In this unit we think about some of the things that could be done to make our roads safer.

Car crime

Accident report

It was 7.45am, and just getting light, when Sadie, aged 13, started to cycle home after finishing her paper round. About half a mile from her house, on the busy London Road, Sadie was hit by a car and knocked off her bike. She was taken to hospital with serious injuries.

The car driver, Warren Taylor, told the police that he thought he was doing 'about 45 mph' in what was a 40 mph zone. From the tyre marks left on the road, the police estimate that Warren's speed was nearer to 50 mph. A witness said she thought that the car was travelling at the same speed as the rest of the traffic. She also said that she believed that the car driver was using a mobile phone.

Sadie had no lights on her bike, nor was she wearing a crash helmet.

Warren said that he had needed to make an important call to someone at work. He said that, at the time of the accident, he was on a straight road and in full control of the car, but did not see the girl on the bike. 'It was dark,' he told the police, 'and she hadn't got any lights.'

 THINK! Put yourself in the position of the police officers investigating the accident.
- **What are the important facts of the case?**
- **Who do you think is responsible for the accident? It could be more than one person.**

When their investigation had been completed, the police sent an accident report to the Crown Prosecution Service. These people have the job of deciding whether there is enough evidence for the person to be charged with a criminal offence and for the case to go to court.

The law covering this area is outined in the section opposite.

THINK! Do you think any of the people involved should be charged with an offence? If you think they should, what would the offence be?

The law

Speeding: It is an offence to go above the speed limit set for a particular area. It is no excuse for drivers to say that they didn't realise they were going so fast or that they were not causing any danger.

(40)

Careless driving: is to drive without proper care and attention.

Dangerous driving: is to drive in a way that is far below the standard of a careful driver, and in a way that the driver should realise is dangerous.

Cycle helmets: there is no law in Britain that requires a cyclist to wear a crash helmet. They are compulsory in some other countries, such as Australia.

Lights: it is an offence to ride a bicycle without a front and rear light and a rear reflector when it is dark, or when there is reduced visibility.

Motoring offences

When someone is found guilty of a crime, the judge or the magistrates have to decide what should happen to that person.

Most offences carry a range of possible punishments. It is the job of the judge or magistrate to decide what they feel is the fairest way of treating a person who is found guilty.

Rebecca, aged 11, was knocked down and killed when she was hit by a car. At the time of the crash the driver was using his mobile phone. He admitted careless driving, and was fined £250.

Arthur, aged 79, was killed when he was involved in a collision with an on coming car. The driver of that car had pulled out to overtake at 70 mph, while talking to her boyfriend on her mobile phone. She admitted dangerous driving and was jailed for 12 months and banned from driving for two-and-a-half years.

? Questions ?

1 How seriously should the courts treat motoring offences? Should a driver who knocks down and kills someone in the road be treated in the same way as a person who kills someone in a fight?

Driving lessons

Safer roads

* in a year

Number of deaths *		Number of deaths per 100,000 people *	
Austria	1,079	Austria	13.4
Belgium	1,364	Belgium	13.4
Denmark	500	Denmark	9.4
Finland	427	Finland	8.3
France	8,487	France	14.4
Germany	7,749	Germany	9.4
Great Britain	3,423	Great Britain	5.9
Greece	2,131	Greece	20.3
Irish Republic	472	Irish Republic	12.8
Italy	6,724	Italy	11.7
Luxembourg	60	Luxembourg	14.3
Netherlands	1,090	Netherlands	7.0
Portugal	2,730	Portugal	28.9
Spain	5,319	Spain	13.5
Sweden	570	Sweden	6.4

Figures collected by the Organisation for Economic Co-Operation and Development, 1999

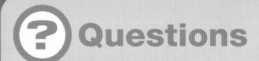 **Questions**

Look at the information in the table above

1 Which country has the greatest number of road deaths?

2 In what position does Great Britain come?

Now look at the chart showing the deaths per 100,000 people:

3 Which countries have the highest and lowest figures?

4 The day that these figures were released, some members of the government were reported as saying that Britain now has the safest roads in Europe. Why did they say it and do you think it is a reasonable claim to make?

A change in the law?

The laws controlling traffic on our roads have changed greatly over the last 150 years. Whenever a new law is passed there is always a lot of argument over whether it is a good or bad idea.

1865 The 'Red Flag' Act requires cars to be driven by three people, with one of the people walking ahead carrying a red flag. Speed limits are 4 mph in the country and 2 mph through towns.

1896 Many parts of the 'Red Flag' Act are changed. No one is now required to walk in front of the car and the speed limit is raised to 14 mph.

1903 Speed limit raised to 20 mph.

1930 The 20 mph speed limit is abolished and a minimum age of 17 is introduced for car drivers.

1935 30 mph speed limit introduced in towns.

1965 70 mph speed limit introduced on motorways.

1967 The breathalyser test is introduced, measuring the amount of alcohol in a driver's bloodstream.

1973 Motorcyclists are required to wear crash helmets.

1975 The first 'sleeping policemen' - raised strips in the road designed to reduce traffic speed – are introduced.

1983 Drivers and front-seat passengers in cars fitted with seat belts are required to wear them by law.

1987 All cars to be fitted with rear seatbelts.

1989 All children under 14, travelling in the back of a car, to wear seatbelts.

1991 All rear seat passengers to wear seatbelts.

1992 Roadside speed cameras are used for the first time in Britain.

Since the early 1980s the number of deaths and injuries on this country's roads has steadily fallen. In France, where the number of road accidents is very high, the French Government has tried to introduce some of the same laws as we have in Britain.

The Government has said that, by the year 2010, it wants to halve the number of road accidents in which children are involved. If it is to do this it will probably need to make some more changes in the law.

5　What makes the roads dangerous for children?

6　What steps can you suggest might make our roads safer for children?

All in the game

In this unit we look at the question of safety in sport.

Sports injuries

Foul!

Imagine you are in a large shop looking for some new clothes. The shop is being re-fitted and parts have been closed off. As you step back from a display you feel a sharp blow on your leg. A worker is carelessly carrying a bucket and painting materials and has hit you. He doesn't seem to notice and walks off. Your leg is hurting and you notice that your trousers are now filthy.

Compare that situation with what would happen on the sports field if you got a similar blow on the leg. The chances are that you would get up, rub your leg, and get on with the game.

The law

A sports injury is not quite the same as an injury you might receive from a person in the street. The law says that if you agree to play a contact sport, you must accept any knocks or injuries that are a *normal* part of the game.

Referee!

During a Scottish League match between Glasgow Rangers and Raith Rovers, the referee blew his whistle for a foul. In dealing with this, he failed to notice one of the Rangers' players, Duncan Ferguson, head-butt a member of the opposing team. However, the incident was clearly seen by the millions watching the match on television.

> **THINK!** **What should happen to Duncan Ferguson? Should what he did be treated as part of the game, or as an assault (which is a crime)?**

The Scottish Football League banned Duncan Ferguson from playing for 12 games but he was also sentenced to three months' imprisonment by a court. The judge said that 'such criminal acts cannot be tolerated on the field of play any more than ... in any place in this country.'

? Questions

1 What are the differences between accidentally being hurt in a shop and on a sports field?

2 What would you say to someone who was always complaining about getting hurt in games where physical contact is allowed?

3 At what point does a sporting foul stop being just part of the game?

The unexpected

Ben Smolden, aged 17, was playing in a game of rugby that was bad-tempered and getting out of hand. Added to this, the scrum kept collapsing, increasing the chance that someone would get hurt. The linesman warned the referee that something ought to be done. But nothing changed. Eventually, when another scrum collapsed Ben ended up underneath a pile of bodies and his back was badly hurt. So much so, that he was permanently paralysed.

Ben Smolden took the referee to court and sued him for damages. The judge said that referees have a legal duty to make sure that the players are reasonably safe and that, in this case, the match had not been properly refereed. The referee was ordered to pay Ben a large sum in compensation.

Seeing red

Eric Cantona was playing for Manchester United in a match against Crystal Palace in January 1994, when he was sent off for kicking out at a Palace player. As he was walking towards the dressing room, Mathew Simmons ran down to the front of the crowd and started shouting at Cantona.

Simmons gave Cantona a torrent of abuse, telling him in a most obscene and racist way to leave England and to go back to France. When Matthew Simmons was asked for his version of the story he said that he had walked eleven rows down to the front and simply said, 'Off, off, off. Go on Cantona. Have an early shower.'

What is agreed, however, is that Cantona reacted by leaping over the advertising hoarding, and landing a two-footed kick on Simmons' chest.

All in the game

Risky business

Watch it!

Having fun is something everyone wants to do, and part of having fun may be taking risks. Lots of sports, like skiing, hang-gliding or motor racing, involve risks and this helps to make them exciting. So whose fault is it when a skier has an accident? The answer is, it depends. In many cases the only people who are at fault are the skiers themselves. But if a skiing instructor sends someone down a slope that is too difficult for them, that is different.

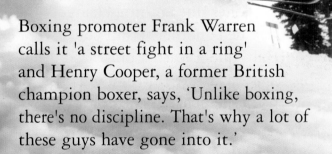

! **THINK!** Are there any sporting activities you would ban because they are too dangerous? Why?

Anything goes

In February 2000, at a Milton Keynes leisure centre, in front of a large crowd Lee Hasdell, a large man weighing 100 kg, flung his weaker opponent to the floor. He dived on top of him, locking his legs around the man's neck in a tight strangle-hold. At the same time he was punching the man into submission.

This is a new sport called total fighting. In total fighting anything is allowed, except eye gouging, biting, hitting your opponent in their groin or their throat, or bending back their fingers. Should it be allowed? Some people think not.

Boxing promoter Frank Warren calls it 'a street fight in a ring' and Henry Cooper, a former British champion boxer, says, 'Unlike boxing, there's no discipline. That's why a lot of these guys have gone into it.'

Critics of the sport say it is not properly controlled. Boxers have to have brain scans once a year but total fighters are not protected in this way. Lee Hasdell, on the other hand, says total fighting is safer than boxing because the head is not the main target.

? **Questions**

1 Members of the local council in Milton Keynes had to decide whether to allow a total fight to be held in the town. What are the arguments for and against allowing the fight to go ahead? What do you think the council should do?

2 Do you think total fighting comes into the same category as boxing?

3 Recently newspapers have reported an increase in boxing in schools. Some people believe boxing is 'character forming'. Do you agree? What would your reaction be if people under 18 were banned from boxing?

Almost all the Milton Keynes council members agreed to let the fight go ahead. Only one person expressed serious doubts. That was Councillor Roy Miller, who decided to abstain from the vote. 'I'd like to see a fight for myself,' said Councillor Miller, 'before saying whether it should be banned, and I think I shall be watching the audience as much as the fighters themselves.'

Sporting chance

In June 1998, Jane Couch became the first woman boxer to be allowed to fight in Britain. Jane gave up her job in a factory making Blackpool rock to become a boxer, but had to fight abroad at first because the British Boxing Board of Control would not let her box in Britain.

Jane, who is now the World Welterweight Champion, took the Boxing Board of Control to court on grounds of sex discrimination and won her case.

When it was all over she said, 'It's just a relief and I'm glad I can now show everyone in this country what a good fighter I am.' The Boxing Board of Control said that they supported equal rights for men and women, but did not think women should box, because of the harm that it could do to them.

4 Here are some of the arguments that the Boxing Board of Control probably thought about when they were trying to come to a decision. Which of the arguments do you agree with? How far do you agree with each one?

a) Women are supposed to be the gentler sex. Boxing gives them a bad image.

b) It should be up to women, not men, to decide whether they fight in the ring.

c) Women's bodies are not suited to a sport of this kind – so they shouldn't be allowed to do it.

d) Everyone should be free to do what they want unless it brings harm to other people.

e) Unlike men, women are not naturally aggressive. Therefore they don't need to do this kind of thing.

5 Do you think women should be prevented from boxing or wrestling?

Index and keywords

Index

A
Alcohol **26**
Animals
- buying a pet **26**

B
Bullying **6, 30-33**

C
Charities **8**
Children
- at work **46-51**
- babysitting **49**
- giving evidence in court **26**
- in care **5**
Cigarettes **27**
Consumer safety **52-5**
Crime **34-45**
- racist **42-5**
Criminal responsibility
- age of **17, 24-5, 34-6**

E
Education
- at home **6,7**
- duty to provide **5**
- history **8**
- home-school agreement **12-3**
- 'otherwise' **7**
- welfare officer **5**

F
Film and video **26**
Fireworks **26, 55**

G
Gambling **26**

H
Health
- medical treatment **26, 28-9**
- records **26**
Home
- leaving home **26**
Human rights
- European Convention on
Human rights **23**
- Human Rights Act 1998 **11**
- in school **11**

L
Local authority care **5**

M
Marriage
- minimum age **25**
Motor vehicles
- driving licence **27**
- safety **54, 56-9**
- seat belts **27, 59**

P
Parents
- children **16-23, 49**
- children's education
5-7, 12, 13
- corporal punishment **18-23**
- home-school agreement
12, 13
- parental responsibility **19, 26**
- rights and duties
**5, 7, 16-21, 26, 27,
29, 35, 49**
Passport **27**
Police
- powers **5**
Politics **25, 27**
Punishment
- corporal **18-23**

R
Racism **42-5**
Road safety **56-9**

S
School
- attendance **4-5, 8, 9, 27**
- bullying **6, 30-33**
- exclusion **11**
- governors **11**
- home-school agreements
12, 13

- human rights **11**
- leaving **27**
- punishment **8**
- records **27**
- rules **10-12, 14-5**
- safety **14, 15, 30-31**
- year **9**
Sex
- age of consent **27**
- contraception **27**
- homosexuality **27**
Sport
- dangerous **62-3**
- violence in **60-61**

T
Truancy **4, 5**

V
Voting
- minimum age **25, 27**

W
Work
- babysitting **49**
- children working **27, 46-51**
- minimum wage **46**
- part-time **27, 47**
- safety **49-51**
- wages **46-7, 50-51**

Cross-referenced keywords

A
Age of criminal responsibility **35**
Attendance Centre **33**

B
Barrister **15**
Blackmail **33**
By-laws **49**

C
Charities **9**
Compensation **15**
Compulsory **9**
Convictions **35**
Corporal punishment **23**

D
Damages **53**

E
Educational psychologist **5**
European Court of
Human Rights **23**
Exclusion **11**

G
Governors **11**
Grievous bodily harm **43**

I
In care **5**

J
Jury **23**

L
Law Lords **53**
Local authority **15**

M
Magistrate **55**

P
Probation **35**
Prosecute **45**

S
Sue **53**

T
Trading standards
department **55**

V
Voluntary **9**

Y
Young offender institution **33**